BLACK AGGIE

THE ORIGIN, HISTORY, AND FOLKLORE
OF BALTIMORE'S MOST FAMOUS GHOST STATUE

MATT LAKE
ILLUSTRATED BY RYAN DOAN

BLACK AGGIE IN THE MIRROR

Baltimore and the towns around it cherish
two separate memories of the legend known
as Black Aggie.

This little book celebrates both.

We begin with the first — a spirit that you
can summon in the mirror, like Bloody Mary.

This little section is a memoir from the kind
of typical sleepover that could have happened
anytime between the 1950s and a couple of
years ago. What follows recreates an
incident that happened
in the 1980s.

You can't remember who made the suggestion first, but before you knew it, there was a plan. You were going to summon the spirit from the Other Side.

So everyone attending the slumber party crowded into the bathroom and stared at the mirror. You all knew the chant, but at first, there was silence. The giggles that had passed around the room when you first talked about the spirit were long gone. And she...well, she was lurking somewhere near, on the edge of the spirit world, waiting to hear her name.

All you had to do was say that name three times, and then she would appear. You would see her, standing behind you in the mirror... a dark presence, her face half covered by a shroud but with eyes glowing from the shadows...and she would take someone in the room. You could only pray it wouldn't be you.

And so there you stood, and the chant began, faintly at first...

"BLACK AGGIE!

...then louder...

BLACK AGGIE! .

..and louder still...

BLACK AGGIE!"

And the next thing you know, everyone in the bathroom pushed past you—rushing to get out—and the last one to leave the room flicked the light switch off and slammed the door behind her—and you were plunged into darkness, alone, and as you groped in pitch blackness of the windowless room and grabbed the handle of the door... it was stuck! The door that was your only way out wouldn't open! It was being blocked by some force too strong for you to overcome.

And then you heard the laughter from the other room. You hadn't summoned Black Aggie that night. You'd been pranked by your friends. It was they who were blocking the door. And then they let you out, laughing with a hint of nervousness. No harm, no foul. You were all friends after all. And as always, after your fear had died down, you would laugh along with them.

This wouldn't be the only time you and your friends would seek out Black Aggie. Oh, no. You'd grow up a bit, learn how to drive, and you'd get together again, and someone would speak of her again. This time, you'd all get into a car and drive to her place.

But all of this would come later.

"LET ME TELL YOU ABOUT BLACK AGGIE..."

Black Aggie is the name given a statue that used to sit
in the Druid Ridge Cemetery in Pikesville, Baltimore County.

Although newspaper articles and books mention the
history and legends and shenanigans that
surround this statue, the most important tales
were whispered among teenagers looking for thrill
rides on dark summer nights.

These tales were passed down through generations
by word of mouth.

This section reproduces verbatim some of the oral history
related to Black Aggie, as recorded in the late 1960s.

Such stories are still being told today.

In a box in the Folklore Archive at the University Of Maryland College Park campus lie the transcripts of an oral history project conducted during an English class in the 1960s. They contain many variants of one of Baltimore's most treasured folk legends— the dark statue in Druid Ridge Cemetery that comes to life in order to kill. The statue is known as Black Aggie.

Like all real folklore, the tales of Black Aggie don't line up into a tidy narrative. As storytellers have retold the tale over the years, certain details have been accepted as canon fact—and real historical research has been applied to get to the bottom of the tale.

This, of course, misses the point completely. When people go out into a cemetery at night for a good scare, they don't care about factual accuracy or narrative consistency: They care about getting the pulse racing. And these are some of the tales they told, in the words of college students from Baltimore, transcribed in the late 1960s in an English class, and archived in a library in College Park.

The box is labeled with this announcement:

THE FOLLOWING MATERIAL IS TO BE LEASED TO THE MARYLAND UNIVERSITY FOLKLORE ARCHIVE AND MAY BE SUBJECT TO PUBLIC USE AND/OR PUBLICATION.

In the event of the publication of any item, it is requested that the informants' names be withheld.

In accordance with the wishes expressed in UMD's license, we are redacting the names and identifying markings from all of these oral histories. Except for that, these tales are reproduced here exactly as those students told each other more than fifty years ago.

They say that if you sit in her lap at midnight, you can hear her heart beating. Some people have seen her move. She used to have green emerald eyes, but they had to remove them because they were too scary.

OF MARYLAND

February 9, 1935

MONDBACK

UNIVERSITY OF MARYLAND   MON., MARCH 18, 1968

pends $3500

chines

She is a big bronze statue at the Druid Ridge
Cemetery. Everyone calls her Black Aggie but
she is really green. She looks like a shrouded
angel, very spooky at night. About four years
ago, a man cut her hand off. They had found
this girl early in the year, stabbed through
her heart. This man swore he didn't know how
the severed arm got into the trunk of his car.

People say that the man saw Black Aggie murder
the girl with her knife and was going to make
sure that Aggie never stabbed anyone again. He
told his story to the judge, but the judge didn't
believe him. The judge made him restore the hand.
Someone had almost stopped Black Aggie, but she
got her power back.

She's a statue of an old colored lady with a baby in her arms. This old colored lady's baby was killed by white people in some crazy way. Now the statue puts a curse on any white person who goes out there and looks at her.

Once as a joke a fraternity took a boy out to see her, made him sit on her lap, and dropped a piece of raw liver down the pledge's back. He died of fright.

got her power

MONDBACK

UNIVERSITY OF MARYLAND   MON., MARCH 18, 1968

pends $3500

February 9, 1935

No plant life will grow anywhere around her.
At midnight when there is a full moon, she will
roll her eyes and raise her hands in anger.

People who have returned the gaze of Black
Aggie's red eyes have been struck blind
instantly. If you are pregnant, do not go
out and see her at night or your child will
be stillborn.

DIAMONDBACK

pends $3500

February 9, 1935

One pledge died there of fright, because the frat boys let him go after he sat in Black Aggie's lap, but they left him there.

When they came back for him, they found him dead. His body was mashed to a pulp. She had wrapped her arms around him and squeezed him to death.

MONDBACK

UNIVERSITY OF MARYLAND   MON., MARCH 18, 1968

pends $3500

hines

February 9, 1935

The reason she is there is because the husband, whose name was Agnus, killed his wife.

He erected this statue as a joke to her. They never caught him for it, though. It was only after he died that it was brought out that he killed her.

Now her ghost haunts the statue. At midnight, you can see her move. Any couple who goes out and parks there is killed.

It is the revenge for what her husband did to her.

If you go to see her with friends of the same sex, you will be alright. You only get killed if you go with a member of the opposite sex.

This started because a boy and a girl went there once and they were doing something they shouldn't have been doing, right there on her lap. So she killed them for revenge.

She doesn't bother you if you are alone, though.

At midnight she sometimes gets up and
wanders around the cemetery.

They have a lake there and she strangles
all the white ducks that live there.

UNIVERSITY OF MARYLAND   MON., MARCH 18, 1968

February 9, 1935

She used to have marbles in her eyes that
light up green. They were stolen.

If you sit in her lap at night, her arms
will come around and squeeze you to death.

It happened to a boy in a fraternity once,
his name was Steve Bledsoe. Before it
happened, he cried out "It's moving,
it's moving." It was during Fraternity
Hell night.

She's a big black statue, but I think she's made of copper...just really dark green copper.

She has eyes made of rubies, and when you look at her at night, it looks like her eyes are bleeding.

If you sit on her lap, you will die.

February 9, 1935

She's sitting on a rock and has a pair of scissors in her hand. If you sit on her lap, she will kill you with the scissors.

They found one girl stabbed to death one morning in her lap.

February 9, 1935

I think that this man built Black Aggie in contempt for his wife. She is at that cemetery out in Pikesville. She's a black statue with green eyes. I went to see it with one of my fraternity brothers. One person in another fraternity died of fright looking at it.

He heard her talking to him, and she's supposed to put a curse on you. He screamed and had a heart attack. That's all I know.

February 9, 1935

I have nothing to tell you. If you want to see the statue, I'll be happy to direct you to her. She is no different than any monument in the cemetery. You had better pick another topic.

I can tell you that the statue is a copy of the original that stands in the Rock Creek Cemetery, marking the grave of Mrs. Henry Adams. Nobody bothers it.

These stories are just a lot of nonsense.

OF MARYLAND

February 9, 1935

MONDBACK

UNIVERSITY OF MARYLAND   MON., MARCH 18, 1968

pends $3500

Atropos, often confused for Black Aggie, in Druid Ridge Cemetery, Pikesville, MD.

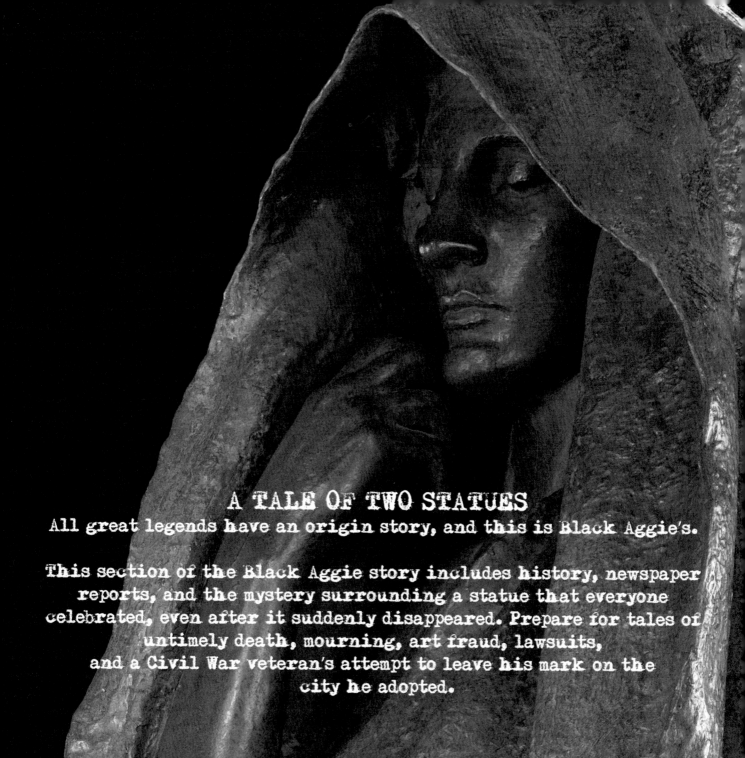

A TALE OF TWO STATUES
All great legends have an origin story, and this is Black Aggie's.

This section of the Black Aggie story includes history, newspaper reports, and the mystery surrounding a statue that everyone celebrated, even after it suddenly disappeared. Prepare for tales of untimely death, mourning, art fraud, lawsuits, and a Civil War veteran's attempt to leave his mark on the city he adopted.

It's fifty years ago, it's night-time, and a car full of thrill-seekers has just reached Druid Ridge Cemetery in Pikesville, Baltimore County.

It's 1967, but they are already the third generation of thrill seekers to see if they can survive an encounter with the notorious haunted statue Black Aggie.

They make their way to Aggie's last known location—a marble slab with the word AGNUS on it. And on the spot where the dark statue sat with her head shrouded and her hand touching her cheek there is now...nothing. Just a scar on the marble where her seat had been.

Black Aggie had left the cemetery—and she's not been seen there since. The mystique surrounding the statue formed the perfect breeding ground for a whole new set of legends. She was already known for coming to life to kill people at her grave site— now, they said, she had come to life and begun wandering the cemetery in search of a whole new set of victims. She might be sitting on another grave, waiting for you to pass her.

In short, all the lurking terror that the writers of Doctor Who put into the supernatural species the Weeping Angels had already germinated, decades earlier, in Baltimore's Black Aggie legends.

But there's a history behind the legends that is by turns tragic, angry, and rife with a particular kind of media-savvy showmanship. And it centers around a charismatic public figure named Felix Agnus.

FELIX AGNUS
Baltimore American.

Brigadier General Felix Agnus was a French-born mercenary soldier who became a diplomat and then a prominent Baltimore newspaperman. He settled in Baltimore after fighting his way across Europe in the mid-1800s and moving to the United States to enlist as a private during the American Civil War.

This scrappy mercenary fought with such distinction that he left military service at the age of 26 as a Brigadier General, but only after being injured multiple times. His newspaper buddy H.L. Mencken would later claim he had so much lead in his body, he would rattle when he walked.

Following one of his injuries, when he was a mere lieutenant, he was taken to Baltimore for treatment. His nurse was Annie Fulton, the daughter of Charles Carroll Fulton, a newspaper magnate who published the Baltimore *American*, and the two became very fond of each other.

When he left the service, he returned to Baltimore to marry Annie and begin a postwar career in the government. He thrived in his new job too, and eventually served as Consul in Ireland for the United States Senate. When he returned to Baltimore, he took the reigns of his father-in-law's newspaper business, which he ran until his death.

When he had secured his fortune, Agnus purchased a family burial plot in one of the city's beautiful garden cemeteries at Pikesville's Druid Ridge. This was common practice in the late Victorian era, and so was the practice of decorating your grave before you died. So around 1905, he commissioned a striking memorial statue for his empty family plot in Druid Ridge Cemetery. The company promised to deliver a striking statue that would be unique to Baltimore—they intended to produce only one such statue per city in the United States, and they charged a premium for it, $3,500. What they delivered was exactly what they promised: An unnerving work of art—a shrouded woman with her eyes closed and one hand up to her face. She seemed to be facing a dark future with grim resolution. And she attracted a lot of interest from the kind of people who loved cemetery art.

The statue also attracted comment from the widow of the famous sculptor, Augustus St. Gaudens, but it was not the kind of comment he would have relished. The widow St. Gaudens said that this was an unauthorized copy of some of her husband's work—and that it wasn't a very good copy either. She pulled no punches in her criticism of General Agnus, saying he "must be a good deal of a barbarian to copy a work of art in such a way."

This was a harsh smackdown for one public figure to issue against another, but the facts seemed to be in the widow's favor.

GRIEF, THE ORIGINAL AGGIE

There was a statue in DC that looked very much like the one that Agnus had installed in his family plot. This bronze went by the long-winded name *The Mystery of the Hereafter and the Peace that Passeth Understanding*, and was also referred to as *The Peace of God.* But most people just called it either the Adams Memorial or *Grief*, because that's the overwhelming sensation viewers took away from the memorial.

Grief had been drawing crowds to Rock Creek Cemetery for fifteen years, and it was located only about forty miles south of Druid Ridge Cemetery. To make things harder on Agnus, the statue was indeed the work of the most famous and best-connected sculptor of his era, and it has been commissioned by Henry

Adams, an influential member of a dynasty of Washington insiders.

1910 photo of St. Gaudens' statue Grief in Rock Creek Cemetery, Washington, D.C.

The Adams family had had an inside track in Washington for more than a century—it had spawned two presidents, John and John Quincy, and several members of the smart social set, including John Quincy's great-grandson, the historian Henry Adams. And it was Henry's wife, the popular hostess Marian Hooper Adams, whose grave featured this amazing statue.

Universally known by her nickname, Clover, Marian Adams had been such a popular figure in Washington social circles that she had inspired two great works of literature during her lifetime—she is widely recognized as the inspiration for the heroines of Henry James's novels *Daisy Miller* and *Portrait of a Lady.* She was also an accomplished pioneering photographer who developed her own film and prints, a bright and creative soul who was the life of every party.

At the age of 42, while she and her husband were building a beautiful new house for the next phase of their lives, she fell into a deep depression. Her father had died in the spring of 1885, and by winter, she was inconsolable. And then she was dead. She was found in her bedroom in early December of 1885, dead of an apparent "paralysis of the heart," but the circumstances were suspicious.

Henry destroyed all her papers and fell reticent about the circumstances of her death. It was widely known that Clover possessed a supply of chemicals for her hobby including the highly toxic potassium cyanide, and all these signs pointed to the cause of her death as suicide.

For the next four years, Henry Adams worked to mark her grave with a suitable memorial, and only after considerable work by the most accomplished sculptor of the time, Augustus St. Gaudens, was the statue revealed. It was immediately praised as St. Gaudens' finest work, and a suitable memorial for a much-beloved woman.

HOW GRIEF BECAME AGGIE

Which brings us back to Baltimore, fifteen years later, and Felix Agnus's public embarrassment at buying a knock-off of a much-beloved statue.

He had in good faith ordered a work of art he knew was a reproduction, but he did not know it was an unauthorized one. The news came out that it was a copy made by a sculptor-for-hire, Eduard Pausch, who made sketches and took measurements of Grief and sculpted his own version of it.

The St. Gaudens estate offered to provide Agnus with an authorized copy of the statue at cost, if he would remove and destroy the original. But Agnus had paid thousands for his statue and he wasn't about to pay thousands more, so he demanded his money back from the company that sold him the copy. They stalled for years until Agnus was forced to sue them for $5,000—a considerable sum in early twentieth century dollars. And he won the lawsuit, which vindicated him in the public eye.

But he kept the statue at his family plot. He buried his mother under its mournful gaze. He buried his wife Annie there too. And a few years after Annie's death, when he himself died in 1925, that's also where he was buried.

It was then, in years that followed, that the legends of Black Aggie began to appear and spread like wildfire.

WHO-STRUCK-JOHN ON AGGIE

Over the next twenty years, a midnight ritual emerged among teenage thrill-seekers. In a social routine that bounced around between dances, drinking, and diners, they would weave in a visit to Druid Ridge Cemetery to seek out the Agnus statue. They would spin yarns like the ones that ended up in the UMD folklore archive, building up a mood of supernatural horror drawn from the Universal Studios horror films Dracula and Frankenstein that were a new craze at the time. They would invent dire tales about the woman buried there to explain why her ghostly spirit was so angry at the living.

Then they would dare each other to sit in the statue's lap.

This sounds like harmless hijinks at first, but it was an upsetting ritual for the cemetery and the Agnus family. The visitors did not always leave the place as they found it. Shrubbery was routinely trampled. Trash was scattered around. On several occasions, they left marks on the statue. By the beginning of 1950, matters had reached a head, and the cemetery company planted a story in Baltimore's *Evening Sun* that called these visits a "desecration" and warned that police patrols would apprehend any night-time revelers.

In the article, a Pikesville police officer offered the statement "There are a lot of stories. The kids say the eyes shine in the dark and things like that. But that's a lot of who-struck-John."

(*Who-struck-John* was a popular slang term from the time, meaning nonsense or mischief.)

Detail from a January 1950 article in Baltimore's Evening Sun newspaper

This warning didn't deter thrill-seeking Black Aggie pilgrims from their quest, and it didn't deter less fun-loving visitors either. In fact, one night in 1962, the statue was subjected to criminal vandalism. Somebody sawed off the arm under cover of darkness and removed it from the cemetery. The authorities mounted a thorough investigation and a discreet informant led the police to Dundalk, where they found the severed arm in the trunk of a local metal worker's car.

When he was charged with the crime, the accused said he had no idea how the arm came to be in his car, and suggested that Black Aggie may have cut it off her self in a fit of grief.

The judge didn't buy that excuse, and ordered the man to pay restitution and repair bills. But the story did feed into the lore surrounding the statue. To some, the cemetery vandal became a folk hero: He was hailed as the man who cut off the statue's arm to protect visitors from Black Aggie's death-grip.

SUMMER OF LOVE, NOT AGGIE

After more than four decades of night-time ritual visits to Druid Ridge

Cemetery, the situation had become intolerable to the Agnus family and cemetery company alike. And so it was that in the spring of 1967, the statue was removed. Because of its historic interest, it was donated to the National Collection of Fine Arts, a division of the Smithsonian Institute.

The Agnus memorial as it stands today, with a scar where Black Aggie once sat.

The Smithsonian promptly put it in storage. As an unauthorized copy of an original work, it wasn't the kind of thing they could display to the public. Whenever anyone made inquiries, a spokesman would repeat the party line, using details like these from a 1976 newspaper article:

"We have 15,000 works of art in the museum, and of course we can't display them all. We have another on display in one of our courtyards. It's an original casting and not a copy."

So the celebrated Black Aggie statue was gone for good. But that doesn't mean her legend stopped there. Where facts leave a vacuum, fantasy rushes in twice as strong, and the legend takes another turn.

AGGIE LIVES ON

When you have a legend as tenacious as the Black Aggie, removing the statue won't erase the legend.

People went out at midnight as usual, looking for a statue that comes to life, and when they came to the spot marked AGNUS, all they found was a marble platform with a scar on it where the statue should be.

Clearly, Black Aggie had come to life and was wandering the cemetery in search of new victims. Sometimes she was accused of killing the waterfowl that swam on the cemetery's pond. Sometimes, she was accused of sitting in wait at another cemetery plots. You can't keep a good legend down.

Even before the statue was removed, people were mistaking a second statue for Aggie herself. Some of the oral history records of Black Aggie mention that her hand is outstretched and she is holding a pair of scissors. This is clearly a description of another statue, one representing the Greek legend of Atropos—one of the three Fates who measure out the lives of mortals and cut them off at the end of their time.

Atropos's statue sits a couple of blocks over from the Agnus memorial in Druid Ridge Cemetery. She is mostly intact even to this day—except for a few snapped-off parts of the garland she is holding next to her scissors, ready to cut off another life. And it is she who many people confuse for Black Aggie when they visit Pikesville today.

You *really* can't keep a good legend down: this is far from being the end of the story.

AGGIE GOES TO WASHINGTON

The last we heard of the actual Black Aggie statue was back in the 1970s, when she was sitting in a storage facility operated by the Smithsonian Institute, somewhere in Washington D.C.

The Smithsonian was never going to put a controversial unauthorized statue on display, but they could hardly toss it in a dumpster either. The statue was a gift to the nation from the Agnus family. And periodically, newspapers would call to ask about the final disposition of the statue, usually around Halloween when they were running ghost stories.

The Smithsonian eventually hit upon a plan: They would re-donate the statue to another agency, the United States General Services Administration. They did this in 1987, leaving the problem in somebody else's hands. After decades in mothballs, the statue finally resurfaced. In the 1990s she was installed in an unlikely place: Just around the corner from the White House, in the courtyard of the Dolley Madison House on Lafayette Square.

On the stone plinth where she sits, to the right of her left foot, an explanatory brass plaque describes her provenance. The plaque reads:

> Eduard L. A. Pausch (after Augustus St. Gaudens) Agnus Memorial (after the Adams Memorial) ca 1906-1907. Transfer to the United States General Services Administration, 1987, from the National Museum of American Art, Smithsonian Institution.
>
> Gift of Mrs. Felix Agnus Leser.

Black Aggie sits there now, in a leafy enclave where employees of the Federal Circuit Court of Appeals and tourists alike sit down to take a break for lunch.

You can visit her there, if you like, but the gates to the courtyard are closed at night, so don't expect to relive any of the moonlit Baltimore graveyard rituals, or to experience any of the glowing-eyed terror from Black Aggie's legends.

This dark statue now casts her mournful spell over the lunchtime crowd, but they hardly seem to notice. The real horror of Black Aggie exists where it has always existed, in the fever-dream realm of the imagination, fueled by sleepover mirror-gazing rituals and midnight drives to a dark cemetery forty miles to the north and decades in the past.

PLACES TO GO, SIGHTS TO SEE

ROCK CREEK CEMETERY

The statue that inspired Black Aggie marks the grave of Marian "Clover" Adams. The statue's sculptor, Augustus St. Gaudens, called it *The Mystery of the Hereafter and The Peace of God that Passeth Understanding* but the widower who commissioned it, Henry Adams, wanted it nameless and mysterious. Most people call it *Grief*.

Section E, Lot 202, 201 Allison St NW, Washington, DC 20011

THE SMITHSONIAN

The Smithsonian American Art Museum displays an authorized cast of *Grief*. Henry Adams said the artist "meant it to ask a question, not to give an answer. Like all great artists, St. Gaudens held up the mirror and no more."

American Art Museum, East wing, 2nd floor. 8th & F Streets NW, Washington, D.C.

DRUID RIDGE CEMETERY

The original site of Black Aggie is now an empty marble plinth bearing the name Agnus. But that's not all! Near this is a statue often confused with Black Aggie—a tarnished green statue of the Greek Fate Atropos. One hand reaches out towards you, and in the other she holds a pair of scissors.

7900 Park Heights Ave, Pikesville, Maryland 21208. Annandale Section, Lot 415

DOLLEY MADISON HOUSE

The actual Black Aggie statue sits in the courtyard of Dolley Madison's house, just around the corner from the White House. She was placed there twenty years after being removed from Druid Ridge Cemetery, where nobody can get to her at night to sit in her lap.

Dolley Madison House, 1520 H Street at the corner with Madison Place, Washington, DC.

FIRST CALL PARANORMAL & ODDITIES MUSEUM

Do you dare to sit in Aggie's lap? In 2022, a replica of the statue appeared in this museum, where the staff will encourage you to sit in her lap and pose for photographs.

202 Congress Avenue, Havre de Grace, MD 21078